Sermon Outlines for Revival Preaching

Sermon Outlines for Revival Preaching

James H. Bolick

BAKER BOOK HOUSE
Grand Rapids, Michigan 49506

Copyright © 1964 by Baker Books
a division of Baker Book House Company
P.O. Box 6287, Grand Rapids, MI 49516-6287

Pulpit Library edition
issued December 1986

ISBN: 0-8010-0922-7

Eighth printing, October 1997

Printed in the United States of America

For information about academic books, resources for Christian
leaders, and all new releases available from Baker Book House,
visit our web site:
http://www.bakerbooks.com/

This book is lovingly dedicated to my three precious children:

Lavonne Bolick

Jimmy Bolick

Lana Marie Bolick

They have made my life richer and fuller by their unselfish attitudes and unwavering trust.

FOREWORD

Originality is not claimed for these outlines. These outlines were gleaned from classes in college and Bible Institute; and from many of my preacher brethren, as well as from private study.

These outlines have been used by me in my pastorates and in revival meetings. They are so arranged that the study of God's word will be required to make them useful.

They are sent forth with my sincere prayer that they shall be used of God in bringing souls to Him, and rewards to those who use them.

James H. Bolick

Contents

1. The Ideal Conversion, *Acts 10*   11
2. Deliverance from Sin, *John 5:24*   12
3. From Captivity to Freedom, *I Cor. 10:1–6, 11*   13
4. The Holy Spirit's Mission in a Sinful World, *I Cor. 12:3, 12–13*   14
5. The Purpose of the Cross, *Gal. 1:4*   15
6. Joyful Sounds for Saved Sinners, *Ps. 89:15*   16
7. The Claims of the Son of God, *John 10:30*   17
8. Coming to God for Salvation, *Heb. 7:25*   18
9. The Characteristics of a Spiritual Church, *Acts 2:42–47*   19
10. To Whom Shall We Go? *John 6:53–69*   20
11. Christ, Our Substitute, *Luke 23:13–25, 33*   21
12. God's Bloodhound, *Luke 16:19–31*   22
13. The Depths of Despair, *Job 3:1–3*   23
14. A Cure for Ailing Christians, *Heb. 12:12–15*   24
15. Service for God, *Deut. 10:12*   25
16. The Devil's Brand of Religion, *Matt. 23:27–38*   26
17. Regeneration, *John 3:1–10*   27
18. Walking in the Old Paths, *Jer. 6:16*   28
19. The Sin of Which Most Men Are Guilty, *James 4:12–17*   29
20. Jehovah Jireh, *Gen. 22:1–19*   30
21. Isaiah's Vision of God, *Isa. 6:1–8*   31
22. The Gospel of Abounding Grace, *Rom. 5:20–21*   32
23. The Marks of a Soul-winner, *Acts 8:1–8, 26–40*   33
24. Salvation, *John 14:6; Luke 19:10; Heb. 2:3*   34
25. In Times Like These, *II Tim. 3:1–8; Matt. 24:36–41*   35
26. A Church Using Its Building, *Heb. 12:23–29*   36
27. Love Produced by the Spirit, *Gal. 5:22*   37
28. The Precious Promises of God, *II Peter 1:4; 3:9*   38
29. Nehemiah's Prayer, *Neh. 1:1–2:5*   39
30. The Ministry of Jesus Christ, *Acts 10:34–43*   4

31. The Psalm of Salvation, *Ps. 32:1–11*   41

32. The Death of Lazarus, *John 11*   42

33. Spiritual Power, *Acts 3:1–19*   43

34. Shall We Continue in Sin? *Rom. 6:1*   44

35. Three Classes Among the Lost, *Acts 17:30–32*   45

36. The Supreme Task of the Church, *Mark 16:14–16*   46

37. The Wounds of Jesus, *Luke 24:36–40*   47

38. Positive Salvation, *I John 3:14; II Tim. 1:12; Jude 24*   48

39. The Poverty of God, *Mal. 3:10*   49

40. God's Final Appeal, *Isa. 1:1–20*   50

41. A Glorious Fact, a Tragic Decision, and the Certain Results, *Prov. 29:1*   51

42. Blinded by Satan, *II Cor. 4:3–6*   52

43. The Demands of Discipleship, *John 8:31–32*   53

44. The Greatness of Salvation, *Heb. 2:3*   54

45. Baptism, *Rom. 6:4*   55

46. Honoring God with Our Tithes, *Lev. 27:30*   56

47. The Fact of Christ's Coming, *Acts 1:10–11*   57

48. The Manner of His Coming, *Acts 1:10–11*   58

49. What Will Take Place on Earth After the Rapture of the Church? *I Thess. 4:13–18*   59

50. What Will Happen in Heaven After the Rapture of the Church? *I Cor. 4:1–5; II Cor. 5:9–10*   60

1
The Ideal Conversion
Acts 10

INTRODUCTION. *The subject for our thinking is centered around the first Gentile convert to the church. Others that had been saved thus far were either Jewish, part Jewish, or Jewish proselytes.*

I. THE MAN CORNELIUS. Acts 10:1-2, 22-23.

    A. He was religious. Acts 10:2, "devout" cf. vs. 22.

    B. He feared God. Acts 10:2, cf. Prov. 1:7 "The fear of the Lord is the beginning of knowledge."

    C. He was benevolent. Acts 10:2, "He gave alms."

    D. He was of good report. Acts 10:22.

    E. He was prayerful. Acts 10:2.

    F. He was unsaved. Acts 11:12-14.

II. WHAT WAS LACKING IN HIS LIFE? He had much that was commendable, but he needed two things.

    A. The message of Christ.

        1. He had to hear the message. Acts 11:14, cf. Rom. 10:14, 17.

        2. The message he needed. Acts 10:34-42.

            a. The introduction. Acts 10:34-35.

            b. The life of Christ. vss. 36-38.

            c. The death of Christ. vs. 39.

            d. The resurrection of Christ. vss. 40-41.

            e. The proclamation of Christ. vs. 42.

    B. He had to believe the message and believe in Christ. Acts 10:43. Three elements in saving faith:

        1. Hear and believe the facts. I Cor. 15:2-4.

        2. Decision of the will (repentance). I Thess. 1:9.

        3. Committal to Him. II Tim. 1:12.

III. WHAT HE RECEIVED. Acts 10:43-48.

    A. Remission of sins. Acts 10:43.

    B. The Holy Spirit. Acts 10:44 (Seal — Eph. 1:13-14).

    C. Baptism — "water" symbolic of what had happened.

2
Deliverance from Sin
John 5:24

INTRODUCTION. *The 24th verse of John 5 is the pivot verse of the Gospel of John according to many Bible scholars.*

There are three truths that I want us to consider.

I. THE TRUTH CONCERNING REVELATION. "Heareth my Word." The word of Christ is the word of God. John 8:25-29, 40.

   A. To be saved, one must believe what the Word declares about Christ. Rom. 10:17.

   B. What essential truths does the Word declare about Christ?

      1. Declares Him to be God. John 14:6-9.

      2. Declares that He was made sin for us. II Cor. 5:21; I Peter 2:24.

      3. Declares that He arose from the dead and is able to save to the uttermost. I Cor. 15:3-4; Acts 1:11-12; Heb. 7:25.

II. THE TRUTH CONCERNING GOD'S REQUIREMENTS. "Believeth on Him." What is involved in this term?
    It involves repentance of sin and faith in Christ. Acts 20:21.

      1. To be saved, one must repent. Acts 17:30. Repentance means to be willing to turn your back on sin without reservations, cf. Matt. 21:28-29.

      2. To be saved, one must believe on the Lord Jesus Christ. Acts 16:31.

         a. Believe on Him as Saviour, that He paid our sin debt in full. Rom. 6:23.

         b. Believe on Him as Lord. Rom. 19:9-10. Make Him Lord and Master over our lives.

III. THE TRUTH CONCERNING THE RESULTS OF BELIEVING ON CHRIST.

   A. Hath everlasting life. John 3:18, 36; I John 5:12.

   B. Shall not come into judgment or condemnation. Rom. 8:1.

   C. Hath passed from death unto life. Spiritual death, now. Eph. 4:18-19. Eternal death, in the future. Rev. 21:8; 20:14-15.

3
From Captivity to Freedom
I Cor. 10:1–6, 11

INTRODUCTION. *In our Scripture we have a brief sketch of the history of the children of Israel from Egypt to Canaan. The 6th verse declares that these things were our examples. Note verse 11 also. The word "examples" is the Greek word "tupos"; our word "type." A type is a sign or emblem that foreshadows, or represents, something else. The Exodus of the Children of Israel is a type; it pictures our deliverance from the bondage of sin.*

I. THE CONDITIONS THAT PREVAILED. (The Children of Israel in bondage, slaves of Pharoah and Egypt. Exod. 2:23-25. Moses is sent of God to be the deliverer. Exod. 3:4-10.)

    A. Moses demands liberty. Exod. 5:1.

    B. Pharoah refuses. Exod. 5:2.

II. THE COMPROMISES OFFERED. After four plagues, Pharoah offered compromises to Moses. Pharoah offered:

    A. A false religion. Exod. 8:25. Stay in Egypt.

        1. Man cannot serve God in devil's territory. I John 2:15-17.

        2. Moses' answer. Exod. 8:26-27. Three days journey, speaks of resurrection ground. Col. 3:1-3 Rom. 6:1-4.

    B. A compromise religion. Exod. 8:28.

        1. Borderline Christians.

        2. The reason so many backslide, not far enough in, cf. Luke 9:57-62. (Note vs. 59. "Follow me" means to go all the way.)

    C. A closed-mouth religion. Exod. 10:8-11.

        1. "Go ye men," leave your families. Exod. 10:11.

        2. Get saved, but don't witness.

        3. This is contrary to God's will. It is the duty of every Christian to witness. Mark 5:18-19. "Go tell" also duty of every church. I Thess. 1:8, cf. Ps. 126:5-6.

    D. A religion without sacrifice. Exod. 10:24.

        1. Go, but leave your flocks. Leave your material possessions to Satan and the world.

        2. Moses' answer, Exod. 10:26, implies that God could have "all" if He wanted it, cf. II Cor. 9:6, Matt. 6:25, 31-33. God is to be first.

4
The Holy Spirit's Mission
in a Sinful World
I Cor. 12:3, 12–13

INTRODUCTION. *In the world in which we live there are demoniac powers at work which are bent upon creating unprecedented conflict between the church and the world. The "isms" of today are a searing, driving force, seeking to destroy faith in God and His precious Word.*

We have "communism" with its anti-god philosophy, we have "modernism" with its blatant denials of God's real truths; we have "Catholicism" with its pagan doctrines and efforts to establish one religion under the guise of being apostolic, or one true church.

These conditions force us to face our need and seek that which alone can satisfy our need.

I. THE WORLD'S GREATEST NEED IS THE POWER OF GOD.
   A. This is true because of the kind of world in which we live.
      1. It is a sinful world. II Tim. 3:1-13. Classified as "wicked." How wicked?
         a. Wicked enough to harass and persecute every godly man that ever lived. John 16:1-3.
         b. Wicked enough to reject every overture of divine mercy of God's grace. Matt. 27:22-25. Still true today, cf. Prov. 1:23-29.
      2. It is a tottering world. I Thess. 5:1-3.
      3. It is a spiritual-hungry world. John 6:27-35, cf. Amos 8:11-12.
   B. This is true because human power is not adequate for the need of man. John 4:13.

II. THE GREATEST POWER THAT MAN CAN RECEIVE IS THE HOLY SPIRIT.
   A. The Holy Spirit is available. John 16:7-11.
   B. The Holy Spirit will come into our lives on His own conditions. This involves conviction of unbelief, righteousness and judgment.

III. THE HOLY SPIRIT WILL EMPOWER OUR LIVES WHEN WE MEET THE CONDITIONS.
   A. Recognize our emptiness. Matt. 5:3, cf. The satisfied church. Rev. 3:17. We must be empty of self and sin.
   B. Passionately desire the gift of the Holy Spirit. Jer. 29:13.
   C. Ask God for the Holy Spirit. Luke 11:13.

5
The Purpose of the Cross
Gal. 1:4

INTRODUCTION. *On the great day of atonement, the High Priest slew the sacrifice and sprinkled with blood everything in the tabernacle. The blood on the mercy seat meant atonement for sin, and mercy and grace for the worshiper. The blood over the broken law where the mercy seat rested meant that the demands of justice for a broken law was being satisfied, and that God and sinner had been reconciled, and the sinner could now come into the presence of God in peace. So it is in the Cross of Jesus Christ. When He died on the cross, He opened up a new and living way unto God. Heb. 10:19-20.*

I. THE PURPOSE OF THE CROSS WAS TO REDEEM US FROM ALL INIQUITY. Titus 2:14.

    The Blood of Christ redeems us from all iniquity.

    1. Iniquity includes the condition of the heart, whereas, sin is the transgression of the Law, or the deeds committed. Note the two in Romans 3:9-18.
    2. When Christ redeems us from all iniquity He gives us a new nature. II Cor. 5:17.

II. THE PURPOSE OF THE CROSS IS THAT HE MIGHT BRING US TO GOD. I Peter 3:18.

    A. He brings us to God, not as criminals, but as the blood-washed sons and daughters of God. Rom. 8:29.
    B. He brings us into a proper knowledge of God. John 1:18; 6:44-46; 14:6-9.
    C. He brings us into favor with God. Eph. 1:6 Rom. 8:1.

III. THE PURPOSE OF THE CROSS IS TO BRING US INTO SONSHIP WITH GOD. Gal. 4:4-5.

    A. We are familiar with adoption in human relationships. By nature the child has no claims until adopted.
    B. By nature, I had no claim on God until He saved and adopted me. Eph. 2:12 Isa. 53:6.
    C. When adopted, I became an heir of God, a joint heir with Christ. Rom. 8:14-17.

IV. THE PURPOSE OF THE CROSS WAS THAT HE MIGHT DELIVER US FROM THE PRESENT EVIL WORLD. Gal. 1:4.

    A. As long as we are in this body, we are going to be subject to the temptations, the hardships of this hostile world. II Tim. 2:12; John 15:18-19.
    B. Note the prayer of Jesus Christ. John 17:15.

6
Joyful Sounds
for Saved Sinners
Ps. 89:15

INTRODUCTION. *God has spoken to the heart of every person who has been born again through faith in the Lord Jesus Christ. There are many ways in which God has spoken to us. Let us consider the words of God which are to us joyful sounds.*

I. THE SOUND OF SALVATION.
- A. It is only through Christ that God can speak the truth that sets us free from guilt forever. Heb. 1:1-2; John 14:6.
- B. To a sinner, who knows that he is lost, it is the most welcome sound to hear the truth that Jesus saves. I Tim. 1:15.

II. THE SOUND OF SEPARATION. — (This follows salvation.)
- A. We are exhorted to be a separated people. Rom. 12:1-2.
- B. The people of God have always been commanded of the Lord to be a separated people. II Cor. 6:17; 7:1.
  1. God is a jealous God and wants perfect love and complete devotion. Mark 12:29-30.
  2. God is holy and wants His children to be holy. I Peter 1:15-16.

III. THE SOUND OF SERVICE. Only separated people can really serve God. God always calls His own to service, in His own time, according to His own purpose.
- A. The Lord spoke to Samuel when he was very young and called him to service. I Sam. 3:10-21.
- B. The Lord called Isaiah to a definite surrender to a very difficult task. Isa. 6:8-10.
- C. God called Paul in a very unusual way to a task that stirred the world in his day. Acts 9:1-6, cf. Acts 26:14-20.

IV. THE SOUND OF THE SECOND COMING OF CHRIST. — (This is the sound of real blessed hope.)
- A. Our blessed Saviour promised that He would return for the saved. John 14:2-3.
- B. There is nothing that will inspire Christians to live holy lives as much as a firm belief in the imminent coming of the Son of of God. I John 3:3.

(Adapted from a sermon by Dr. Bob Gray, Jacksonville, Florida.)

7
The Claims
of the Son of God
John 10:30

INTRODUCTION. *There are many claims made by man today in every sphere of our society. First, in the commercial world — cars, soap, shampoos, razor blades, pills, etc. Second, in the political world — capitalism vs. communism. Third, in the religious world — Mormonism, Christian Scientists (Mary Eddy Baker), Free Thinkers, Modernism, Jehovah Witnesses, etc.*

Today, I want us to notice the claims that the Son of God has made, and did make when He was here on this earth.

I. HE CLAIMED THAT HE KNOWS YOU. John 2:24-25.
   A. He knows all about man — and what is in man. Rom. 3:9-20, cf. Mark 7:20-23.

II. HE CLAIMED THAT HE CAME DOWN FROM HEAVEN. John 3:13 (He did not come from the Garden of Eden, from Rome, Washington, London, Moscow.)

III. HE CLAIMED THAT HE MUST DIE AND BE RAISED. John 3:14-15.
   A. This is not a look at a miracle working Christ; or a great teacher or a good example.
   B. This was a look of faith at the crucified risen Lord.

IV. HE CLAIMED THAT HE SPOKE THE WORD OF GOD. John 3:34. "I speak the things I see and hear."
   A. Compare with John the Baptist "who was a voice."
   B. Jesus' doctrine was not His own. John 7:16-19, in the human sense — but in the Divine. It is only through Christ that the things of God are made known. John 15:15.

V. HE CLAIMED THAT HE WAS GIVING THE HOLY SPIRIT WITHOUT MEASURE. John 3:34.
   A. He was conceived by the Holy Spirit. Matt. 1:18.
   B. His entire life was spirit-controlled.
   C. We, who know His name, ought to be controlled by the Holy Spirit.

VI. HE CLAIMED THAT ALL THINGS WERE GIVEN INTO HIS HANDS. John 3:35.
   A. Our salvation is in His hands. Acts 4:12, cf. John 10:27-30.
   B. Our destiny is in His hands. John 5:22-24. He has already revealed what will happen to us.
      1. The believer. John 5:24.
      2. The unbeliever. II Thess. 1:7-9, cf. II Thess. 2:11-12.

8
Coming to God
for Salvation
Heb. 7:25

INTRODUCTION. *Salvation is a doctrine peculiar to Revelation. Salvation can only be found in a person; the way of salvation can only be found in the Scriptures. II Tim. 3:15; I Cor. 1:21.*

Our text teaches the way of salvation. Consider two truths that are taught in this verse.

I. THE PEOPLE WHO ARE TO BE SAVED. (Those who come to God through Jesus Christ. There is no denominational limit mentioned here.)

A. First, note to whom they are to come. "To God."
   1. Coming to church is not coming to God.
   2. Formal worship is not coming to God. Matt. 15:7-9.
   3. Doing good works is not coming to God. Matt. 7:21-23.

   B. What is coming to God? What does it imply?
   1. Coming to God implies leaving something.
      a. Leaving our sins. Isa. 55:7; Luke 13:3, 5.
      b. Leaving our righteousness. Note two things:
         (1) Men are prone to trust their own righteousness. Prov. 20:6; 30:12; 14:12.
         (2) Our righteousness is an abomination before God. Luke 16:15. Therefore, they are unclean, Isa. 64:6, and unprofitable. Isa. 57:12.
   2. Coming to God implies faith in God. Heb. 11:6.

   C. How do men come to God? "By Christ." John 14:6.
   1. This brands the naturalist and the modernist wrong.
   2. This truth declares that there is a mediator between God and man. I Tim. 2:5-6. There is no by-passing Him. Acts 4:12.

II. THE MEASURE OF THE SAVIOUR'S ABILITY. Heb. 7:25 ("He is able to save to the uttermost.")

   A. To the uttermost extent of guilt. Matt. 11:28-30. Chief of sinners. I Tim. 1:15.

   B. To the uttermost of rejection. Neh. 9:26-28.

   C. To the uttermost of despair. Psalm 42:5.

9
The Characteristics
of a Spiritual Church
Acts 2:42–47

INTRODUCTION. *In this passage we have a kind of lightning summary of the characteristics of the early church. This early church was a spiritual church. I believe that our definition of a spiritual church is very different from that which the Bible, God's word, sets forth.*

That the early church was a truly spiritual church there can be no doubt. In the first thirteen chapters of Acts there are more than forty references to the Holy Spirit. The early church was a spirit-filled church.

I. THE HOLY SPIRIT WAS THE SOURCE OF ALL GUIDANCE.
   A. He moved Philip to contact the Ethiopian Eunuch. Acts 8:29.
   B. He prepared Peter for the coming of the emissaries of Cornelius. Acts 10:19. He ordered Peter to go with them. Acts 11:12 (The break-through of racial pride and barriers.)
   C. He ordered the church to set apart Paul and Barnabas to take the gospel to the Gentiles. Acts 13:3-4.
   D. He guided the church in its decisions in the council at Jerusalem. Acts 15:28.

II. ALL THE LEADERS OF THE CHURCH WERE MEN OF THE SPIRIT. (This is the one requirement that we would do well to consider when choosing leaders.)
   A. The seven helpers (deacons). Acts 6:3.
   B. Stephen, the first martyr. Acts 7:55; Barnabas, a faithful servant. Acts 11:19-24.
   C. The elders of Ephesus. Acts 20:28.
   D. All the members of the church. Acts 4:31.

III. THE SPIRIT WAS THE SOURCE OF DAY TO DAY COURAGE AND THE POWER OF THE EARLY BELIEVERS.
   A. The disciples were to receive power when the spirit came. Acts 1:8. They did as is evidenced by witnessing. Acts 2:1-6.
   B. Peter's courage and eloquence before the Sanhedrin is the result of the activity of the Holy Spirit. Acts 4:8-13.
   C. Paul's conquest of Elymas in Cyprus was due to the power of the Spirit. Acts 13:4-12.

IV. OUR NEED TODAY CAN BE MET BY THE HOLY SPIRIT. Eph. 5:18.

10
To Whom Shall We Go?
John 6:53–69

INTRODUCTION. *Most every one has someone to whom they turn for advice. In time of sickness, they seek the advice of a doctor; in legal matters, they seek the advice of a lawyer. But there are some things for which man does not have the answer. As we face eternity with a never dying soul, to whom shall we turn?*

I. TO WHOM SHALL WE GO WITH OUR SINS?
   A. Shall we go to some outstanding man of wealth? Ps. 49:7.
   B. Shall we go to some modernistic positive thinking preacher, who would try to get us to forget our sins by covering them with a change of thinking? Prov. 28:13. (The sinner is negative.)
   C. Shall we go to some earthly priest and confess them? I Tim. 2:5.
   D. Shall we go to Calvary, to Christ who said, "Come unto Me"? Matt. 11:28-30.
      1. It is a fact that Christ died for our sins. Isa. 53:6; Acts 4:12; I Cor. 15:3.
      2. It is a fact that if we refuse or fail to come to Him, we shall die in our sins. John 8:21, 24.

II. TO WHOM SHALL WE GO FOR INWARD PEACE?
   A. The sinner has no peace and there is no peace to be found in the pleasures of sin. Isa. 57:20-21.
   B. True peace is to be found only in Jesus Christ. John 14:27, cf. Isa. 48:18. This peace became possible at a great price. Col. 1:20. So easy to receive. Rom. 8:1.

III. TO WHOM SHALL WE GO FOR ASSURANCE AND SECURITY?
   A. Not to our own opinion alone. Prov. 14:12.
   B. Not to some religious pretender. II John vs. 7.
   C. We *can* go to Christ Jesus for assurance and security. John 10:27-29.

IV. TO WHOM SHALL WE GO WHEN LIFE'S DAY CLOSES?
   A. This depends entirely upon our decision for or against Christ. If we have accepted Him, we can rest upon Psalm 23:4.
   B. If we have rejected Him, we can be sure of an eternal burning hell. Matt. 7:21-23.

11
Christ, Our Substitute
Luke 23:13–25, 33

INTRODUCTION. *In our Scripture, Barabbas was released because Christ took his place, and that by the wicked choice of the people, although behind the act of man we see the hand of God's purpose. We all, by our sins, were parties to Christ's crucifixion. His death was no accident; it was an accomplishment of divine intent, therefore, He was a substitute in many respects.*

I. HE WAS THE GOD-PROVIDED SUBSTITUTE. Rom. 5:8.
   A. God provided His Son as our substitute because He loved us. John 3:16.
   B. Christ "died for us." This death was under the divine wrath of God. Rom. 8:32.

II. HE WAS THE SIN-MADE SUBSTITUTE. II Cor. 5:21.
   A. He was made "sin for us"; lit., He became everything we are. Every sin that we have committed, Christ became. I John 2:2.
   B. The Word makes it plain that He had no sin of His own. I Peter 2:21, 22; Heb. 4:15.

III. HE WAS THE CURSE-BEARING SUBSTITUTE. Gal. 3:13.
   (Consider two words in this verse, "redeemed" and "curse".)
   A. There are three Greek words translated by our English words, "bought" or "redeemed."
      1. The first one is *agarazo* which means to buy in the slave market. This word is used in I Corinthians 6:20 — translated "bought" with a price. I Peter 1:18, 19 tells us what the price was — the precious blood of Christ.
      2. The second word is *exagorazo* which means to buy a slave out of (*ex*) the slave market. This word is used in Galatians 3:13 and it means that we are never to be put up for sale again.
      3. The third word is *lutroo* which means that the price has been paid in full and the slave has been set free. We believers are set free from the slavery of sin. Titus 2:14, cf. Rom. 6:17-18; Rom. 6:6, 11-13.
   B. Consider the word "curse." Gal. 3:10-13.
      1. Galatians 3:10 tells us that we are under a curse, because we have broken the law.
      2. Galatians 3:13 tells us that Christ was made a curse for (lit., above) us.
      3. Galatians 3:13 tells us that Christ redeemed us "from," lit., "out from under" the curse.

12
God's Bloodhound
Luke 16:19–31

INTRODUCTION. *There has been a great deal of controversy over hell, but here we have a description that Christ, Himself, gave of hell.*

I. THE MAN WHO WENT TO HELL. (Wealthy and a man of influence.)

II. WHEN HE WENT TO HELL. (At death.)

III. THE GREATEST PUNISHMENT IN HELL.
   A. Separation from God.
   B. Remembrance.

IV. LET US TAKE A TRIP THROUGH THIS PLACE CALLED HELL WITH ABRAHAM AS A GUIDE.
   A. Rich man — remembered his rejection and his good times.
   B. Herod — the faces of the little babies and the cries of helpless mothers.
   C. Herod and Salome — they see the head of John.
   D. Judas, the betrayer of Christ — his lips burn with the betraying kiss.
   E. Pilate — wringing his hands in hell.
   F. Agrippa — almost, but lost.

V. INTERVIEWS IN HELL.
   A. The boy. What do you remember? Mothers prayers, the preachers' sermons, etc.
   B. The girl. What do you remember? A modern mother, a fast life, etc.
   C. Mothers and fathers. What do you remember? A fanatic preacher, a faithful witness, a cold refusal, etc.

VI. WHY THEY WENT TO HELL.
   A. Let us take the rich man.
   1. He did not go because of riches.
   2. He did not go because of his brutal treatment of Lazarus.
   B. Why? Luke 16:29. He would not hear; he would not believe. John 3:18, 36.

(I am indebted to Rev. Ralph Barnard of Winston-Salem, N. C., for this outline.)

13
The Depths of Despair
Job 3:1–3

INTRODUCTION. *In Chapters 1 and 2 of Job, we see a man brought down into the depths of suffering and sorrow. In Chapter 3 we have the words of one given over to the deepest of despair and trouble. Here is the very depths of despair, "To curse the day that I was born." The word "cursed": lit., to bring into contempt; to despise.*

I. JOB CURSED THE DAY HE WAS BORN. The question immediately arises, "Why?"
   A. Because of his sufferings, loss of wealth, children and health.
   B. Because he did not know why these things had come upon him. The opinion of his friends was that he was a hypocrite. The idea of the world is not that of God.

II. MANY WILL LIVE TO CURSE THE DAY THEY WERE BORN.
   A. The Christian.
      1. The child of God that failed to live for God will have cause at the judgment seat to despise the day he was born. II Cor. 5:10-11. "Terror": to be exceedingly afraid. I Cor. 9:27.
      2. The child of God who has compromised the Word of God, the gospel of Christ. I Cor. 9:16, 19. "Woe": an exclamation of grief.
         a. The emphasis is upon "gospel."
         b. If the gospel is not preached, then men will die in their sins. Rom. 1:16-17; II Cor. 4:1-5.
         c. The gospel is being compromised today for: position, prestige, popularity.
   B. The Unbeliever.
      1. Those who reject the Lord Jesus Christ will have cause to curse the day they were born.
      2. Because of the judgment and wrath of God. Rev. 20:11-15.

III. THE APOSTATE OR HYPOCRITE. Matt. 26:24; Mark 14:21.
   A. Judas was an apostate and hypocrite. John 6:70-71. (A deceiver and an accuser.)
   B. Jesus also labeled others with being the very offspring of Satan. John 8:44. Note of what they accused Christ. John 8:39-41.
   C. Note the words of Christ to those who claim love for Him, but offend His followers. Matt. 18:6-7.

(I am indebted to Rev. Cecil Hedgepeth of Thomasville, N. C., for this outline.)

14
A Cure for
Ailing Christians
Heb. 12:12–15

INTRODUCTION. *All that have believed on Christ as Saviour and Lord have become partakers of Eternal Life. The genuine life of faith should never grow old. II Cor. 4:16; Isa. 40:31. The genuine Christian should run the race with patience and with joy.*

Yet in the letter to the Hebrews, we are made aware that Christians grow tired and weary. The picture we are given in Hebrews 12:12, is one who was paralyzed and on the verge of total defeat. There are two forces warring against the believer. These two forces are paralyzing powers and have a paralyzing effect upon the Christian.

I. FIRST, LET US CONSIDER THESE PARALYZING POWERS. Heb. 12:12-13.

    A. External difficulties. Heb. 10:32-34.

        1. The Christians to whom this Epistle was written were subjected to severe persecutions from without. Heb. 10:32.

        2. The believer is forewarned of persecutions. We can expect them. They will come:

            a. To those who live godly. II Tim. 3:10-12.

            b. To those who are true to Christ. John 15:18-21.

            c. Persecution is a common thing for all Christians. I Peter 4:12-16.

    B. Inward weakness and spiritual fatigue. Heb. 12:12.

        1. Drooping hands. Hands speak of works. They had grown slack. Heb. 5:11-14, cf. James 2:14.

        2. Knees speak of running a race. Heb. 12:1. They had grown weary in running the race.

II. SECOND, CONSIDER THE CURE. (How can the exhortation of Hebrews 12:12 be realized?)

    A. By looking unto Jesus. Heb. 12:2.

    B. By submitting unto the training of the Lord. Heb. 12:5-11.

    C. By being exercised by the chastisement from the Lord. Heb. 12:11.

15
Service for God
Deut. 10:12

INTRODUCTION. *Our Scripture text sets before us what God required of Israel. I want to use this passage by applying it to the church. Keep in mind that God is the same yesterday, today and forever.*

What is service? Performance of labor for the benefit of another; or at another's command. Today Christianity has become a mere intellectual assent to certain beliefs, so far as many are concerned. They have embraced the doctrines without the doctrines embracing them. Faith that neither changes a life or causes one to burn some energy for God is not true, saving faith.

Christ makes no apologies in calling for faithful service from all who have accepted Him as Saviour and Lord. John 17:18; Luke 6:46-49. To follow Christ means to labor. John 9:1-4.

I. SERVICE IS DEMANDED BY THE LORD. Deut. 10:12; I Cor. 15:58.

    A. Christ demands of those that follow Him service. John 12:26. (We are more than servants in our relationship. John 15:14-16).

    B. Our service is to be with reverence and fear. Heb. 12:28.

II. SERVICE IS TO BE ACCORDING TO OUR ABILITY.

    A. Service according to talent. Matt. 25:22-23, cf. Luke 19:11-13. All are to serve.

    B. Service is to be for God's glory. I Peter 4:11.

III. SERVICE IS TO BE UNDIVIDED. Luke 16:13.

    A. Israel exhorted to leave all other gods and to serve the True and the Living God. I Sam. 7:3.

    B. Christ answers Satan. Matt. 4:10.

IV. SERVICE BRINGS RESULTS.

    A. Service glorifies God. Matt. 5:16.

    B. Service demonstrates the reality of our Faith. James 2:17-18; I Peter 2:12.

    C. Service brings others to a saving relationship with Christ. I Cor. 9:19-20; Matt. 9:35-38.

16
The Devil's Brand of Religion
Matt. 23:27–38

INTRODUCTION. *This passage of Scripture contains the hardest utterance that ever fell from the lips of the Son of God. In this passage He pronounces "woes" upon the Pharisees and the Scribes. He denounces them for several reasons, beginning with verse 13, but I have chosen to speak to you from verses 27-38. I do so because I believe that these verses furnish an insight into the character of those that were religious, but who were evil to the very core.*

I believe that there are many of the same kind of people within the scope of Christiandom today. In fact, I think that their number is legion, because they are many. I refer to their religion as being the devil's brand; and I do so because the Word of God warrants such a statement. The devil has his own brand of religion, and he has many followers. II Cor. 11:13-15.

Christ, in this passage, reveals their true condition or character.

I. THEIR HYPOCRISY. Matt. 23:27-30.
   A. The character of the hypocrite. vss. 27, 28.
      1. The word means "to play or act out a part." In this case, they were playing a convincing part. v. 27.
      2. He is outwardly pure. v. 28. (In the eyes of man, righteous; in the eyes of God, corrupt.) Cf. I Sam. 16:7; Isa. 55:8-9.
   B. The conduct of the hypocrite. vss. 29, 30.
      1. Pretended to honor the dead prophets. v. 29.
      2. Protested (outwardly) to pass deeds of violence. v. 30.

II. THEIR HERITAGE. Matt. 23:31-33 Christ declared them to be:
   A. The children of the prophet killers. v. 31, cf. II Chron. 36:15-16.
   B. The products of sinful and depraved training. v. 32.
   C. The crystalized rejectors of all righteousness. v. 33.

III. THEIR HELLISHNESS. Matt. 23:34-38.
   A. Their determined course. v. 34.
   B. Their destruction. vss. 37-38. Note three things:
      1. Those to whom He is speaking. v. 37.
      2. Their absolute rejection of Christ. v. 37.
      3. Their doom. Departure of Christ leaves them desolate. Judicially blind. v. 38.

17
Regeneration
John 3:1–10

INTRODUCTION. *Two major problems confront man. These problems are common to all. They are: (1) The problem of death. By nature all mankind is dead in trespasses and sins. Eph. 2:1; I Cor. 15:21-22. This problem is solved by the impartation of the divine life known as regeneration, or the new birth. (2) The problem of guilt. Romans 3:23. Justification is the solution to this problem. Regeneration is of great importance. By regeneration we enter the kingdom of God.*

I. WHAT IT IS NOT — THE NEGATIVE.

  A. It is not baptism.

    1. Scriptures used by those who teach baptismal regeneration. John 3:5, cf. John 4:10, 14; Eph. 5:26. Figure of speech. I Peter 1:23.

    2. If baptism is the same as regeneration, why did Paul make so little emphasis upon it? I Cor. 4:14-15. He had begotten them through the gospel, but he had baptized only a few. I Cor. 1:14-16, cf. John 4:1-2. For an example of Salvation before baptism note Acts 10:44-48.

  B. It is not reformation. Regeneration is not a natural step in man's development; it is the super-natural act of God. Titus 3:5; John 1:11-12.

II. WHAT IT IS — THE POSITIVE.

  A. Regeneration is a spiritual quickening, a new birth. John 3:3-7. Solely of God. James 1:18; II Thess. 2:13.

  B. The impartation of a new and divine life to a dead sinner. II Cor. 5:17; John 5:24.

  C. The impartation of a new nature means that:

    1. Christ now lives in the believer. Gal. 2:20.

    2. God's seed (nature) now abides in the believer. I John 3:9; II Peter 1:4; Matt. 5:20; cf. Rom. 3:21-22. (Unto all — but only upon those that believe.)

    3. The believer is possessor of two natures. Gal. 5:17.

    4. This new nature will cause the believer to live a holy and righteous life. Eph. 4:21-32.

18
Walking in the Old Paths
Jer. 6:16

INTRODUCTION. *Judah was in a backslidden position. Jer. 6:13, 15; Jer. 2:11-13. The church today is in the same condition before God. Many who are truly saved are following the Lord afar off and they have departed from the Old Paths.*

God exhorted Judah to return to the Old Paths and He would give them rest for their souls. We need to return to some Old Paths.

I. RETURN TO PRAYER. Luke 18:1.
   - A. We have many examples in the word of the Lord where the saints of old prayed. Elijah: I Kings 18:36, 37; Moses: Exodus 32:31, 32; II Chron. 7:14.
   - B. Christ commands that we pray. Luke 18:1. God's plan for His people. Matt. 7:7-8.
   - C. The early church was a praying church.
     1. Began in prayer. Acts 1:13-14.
     2. Continued in prayer. Acts 2:42.
     3. Prayed in time of persecution. Acts 4:15-18, 23-31.
     4. Prayed for a member in need. Acts 12:3-5.

II. RETURN TO LOVE. John 13:34-35.
   - A. This is commanded by Christ. John 13:34-35.
   - B. This is the evidence that we are saved. I John 4:20-21.
   - C. This is the evidence that we are friends of Christ. John 15:12-14, 17.
   - D. Our love is to be manifested by our deeds. I John 3:16-19.

III. RETURN TO COMPASSION. (Love for the brethren. Compassion for the lost.)
   - A. Christ again is our example. Matt. 9:35-38. (Compassion — to have bowels yearning; to pity; to put into action.) Luke 19:41 — "He wept aloud." Why? He knew their condition. Luke 13:34-35. They were lost and bound for hell — should cause us to weep. Cause to pray for laborers. Ps. 126:5-6.
   - B. Paul, a Christian, was a man of compassion. Rom. 9:1-3; 10:1-4.

IV. RETURN TO LIVING FOR GOD. Rom. 12:1-2.
   - A. God wants holy people. I Peter 1:14-16.
   - B. Holiness means separation from the filthiness of both the flesh and the spirit. II Cor. 5:17; 7:1, "cleanse ourselves" — fleshly sins; spiritual sins — sins of the spirit.

19
The Sin of Which
Most Men Are Guilty
James 4:12–17

INTRODUCTION. *In this passage of Scripture there is a warning against judging our fellowman; there is a vivid description of the brevity of one's physical life; and thirdly there is a charge of sin of which most of us must plead quilty at one time or another. A close study of verses 15-17 reveal that this sin is inseparably related to the will of God. Not to do God's will is sin. The Bible plainly sets before us some things that God wills for us to do.*

I. WE SHOULD TRUST HIS SON AS SAVIOUR.

A. We know this because:

1. God sent His Son into the world to save the lost. Gal. 4:4-5. Christ's own testimony. Luke 19:10.

2. God gave His Son to die upon the cross to save from sin. John 3:16, 17.

B. It is absolutely necessary to believe on Christ, obeying God's will to be saved. Matt. 7:21-23. Note Christ's discourse with the Jews. John 6:22-29.

II. WE SHOULD LIVE HOLY AND SEPARATED LIVES AFTER WE ARE SAVED.

A. It is God's will that saved people unite with a church through baptism. Mark 16:15-16. (Ill.: Love the church. Acts 2:41.)

B. It is God's will that saved people live a holy life. II Cor. 6:17; 7:1. Separated sins both of the flesh and the spirit.

C. It is God's will that saved people be faithful in their attendance. Heb. 10:22-25.

D. It is God's will that saved people support His work with their tithes. Mal. 3:7-10; I Cor. 16:1-2. To help their fellowman with their alms. I John 3:16-19; Matt. 6:1-4. To worship with their offerings. Exod. 25:1-2; 35:4-5, 29; 36:6-7.

E. It is God's will that we love and seek to restore those who are overtaken in a fault. Gal. 6:1.

CONCLUSION: These are some of the things that God wills that we do. Not to do them is sin.

20
Jehovah Jireh
Gen. 22:1–19

INTRODUCTION. *In this passage we have Abraham calling God by the name "Jehovah Jireh." This is one of the compound names that is given to the Lord in the Old Testament. The name actually means "That God will provide." In the American Standard Version, Gen.* 22:14: *"And Abraham called the name of that place Jehovah-Jireh: as it is said to this day. In the mount of Jehovah it shall be provided."*

To really understand the significance of this name, we need to consider carefully the events leading up to the time when Abraham spoke of God as being "Jehovah-Jireh."

I. THE TEST WITH WHICH GOD TRIED ABRAHAM. Gen. 22:1-2.
   A. God commanded Abraham to offer his son, Isaac, as a burnt-offering. Gen. 22:2.
   B. This incident reveals several things about Abraham.
      1. He had faith that answered to the Word. Gen. 22:1.
      2. He had faith to obey God's Word. Gen. 22:3-6.
      3. He had faith to trust all to God. Gen. 22:7-10.

II. THE PROVISION THAT GOD MADE FOR ABRAHAM. Gen. 22:11-14.
   A. God provided a substitutionary sacrifice which saved Isaac. Gen. 22:11-14.
   B. This sacrifice, Gen. 22:13, was actually a type of Jesus Christ, who is God's sacrifice for all mankind. John 1:29; I Peter 1:19, 20.
   C. Christ Jesus is the supreme sacrifice which put an end to all sacrifice of life and blood for salvation. Heb. 9:11, 12.

III. THE BASIS FOR GOD'S PROVISION (Grace) Gen. 22:8, 14.
   A. God, to forgive sin, must provide a sacrifice for Himself. Gen. 22:8. Sin must be paid for. Rom. 6:23. Death is the only thing that can pay for men's sins. I Cor. 15:3-4; Rom. 3:24-26.
   B. God, to save mankind, must make provision which entailed the giving of Himself. Gen. 22:14.
      1. Man cannot redeem another. Ps. 49:6-7; I Peter 1:18-19.
      2. Man cannot redeem himself. Jer. 2:21-22; Titus 3:5.
      3. God, through Christ, is the only one that can redeem mankind. II Cor. 5:17-21; Rev. 5:9. Have you trusted Him?

21
Isaiah's Vision of God
Isa. 6:1–8

INTRODUCTION. *If I should ask you today, "When was the last time you saw God?" what would your answer be? I am speaking of seeing God with an eye of faith.*

I. ISAIAH SAW THE LORD. Isa. 6:1.

A. When did he see God? Isa. 6:1. In the year that King Uzziah died. Explain why this incident is mentioned. Isaiah had been depending upon this mighty King Uzziah. II Chron. 26:1, 4, 8, 15, 16.

B. Where did he see God? Upon the throne. Isa. 6:1.

   1. The throne of the universe. This is God's rightful place. Cf. Ps. 2:1-4.

   2. Is He seated upon the throne of your heart?

C. What did he see about God? Isa. 6:2-4.

   1. His holiness. Isa. 6:2-3 (note: Seraphims).

   2. His power. Isa. 6:4. The door posts moved. God's power is an active power, power to deliver and keep. I Peter 1:3-5.

II. ISAIAH SAW HIMSELF. Isa. 6:5-8.

A. First, consider his opinon of himself. "Woe is me! for I am undone." Compare this with the opinion of Peter in Luke 5:8 and Paul, I Tim. 1:15. Only when man sees his true condition is he conscious of his need of God.

B. Second, consider his cleansing. Isa. 6:6-7.

C. Third, consider his commission. Isa. 6:8; John 10:28; Mark 16:15, 16.

22
The Gospel
of Abounding Grace
Rom. 5:20–21

INTRODUCTION. *There are two forces at work in the world — Sin and Grace. In verse 21 these two forces are personified and are represented as kings, sitting on their thrones. These two kings have waged continuous warfare against each other, because they belong to entirely different realms. Satan, the devil, placed sin on the throne, while God enthroned grace. Sin seeks to destroy the souls of mankind; while grace reaches out to save the souls of mankind. Both sin and grace are powerful monarchs, but grace is more powerful than sin. Note with me three truths that are set forth in our Scripture.*

I. THE ABOUNDING REIGN OF SIN. "Where sin abounded." There can be no question about the abundance of sin in the world. Sin has abounded through all the centuries and still abounds today.
   A. Sin has abounded in the length of its reign. It is as old as man. Rom. 5:12 (Adam).
   B. Sin has abounded in the scope of its reign. Rom. 3:23. It has touched every life with the exception of Christ. Eccles. 7:20.
   C. Sin has abounded in the nature of its reign. It is the nature of sin to grow.
   D. The law of God reveals the abounding reign and nature of sin. Rom. 5:20; 7:7-8, 12-13. The law did not cause sin; it revealed sin.

II. THE SUPER-ABOUNDING REIGN OF GRACE. Rom. 5:20. Sin abounds in the world, but grace super-abounds. This is shown by the victories of grace over sin.
   A. Paul was an example. From the chief of sinners. I Tim. 1:15, to a laborer for Christ. I Cor. 15:9-10.
   B. Mary Magdalene was an example. From demon possession to one that ministered unto Christ. Luke 8:1-3.
   C. The woman of Samaria was an example. From being an adulteress to being a witness for Christ. John 4:28.

III. THE RESULTS OF THE TWO REIGNS. Rom. 5:21. (The results are seen by contrasting the two.)
   A. Sin reigned unto death.
      1. Sinners are dead while they live. Eph. 2:1-3.
      2. Sin ends this life in physical death. James 1:15.
      3. Sin, for the unbeliever, will also result in eternal death. Rom. 6:23; Rev. 20:14-15; 21:8.
   B. Grace reigns through righteousness unto eternal life. Rom. 5:21.

(Adapted from a sermon by Dr. J. Clyde Turner.)

23
The Marks
of a Soul-winner
Acts 8:1–8, 26–40

INTRODUCTION. *In our text, Acts* 8:35, *we read that Philip "opened his mouth." That is one of the real needs in our churches today; we need to open our mouths for Christ. We open our mouths to eat; to buy and sell; to gossip; and to criticize. But too few of us open our mouths to preach Jesus Christ.*

Many things are indicated of Philip when he opened his mouth to preach Christ. (1) First, it took courage. Only a few days since, Philip had seen his brother in Christ, Stephen, stoned to death for opening his mouth. Had he kept silent, he would not have been mobbed. (2) Second, it indicates spontaneity.

I. THE MAN PHILIP — WHO WAS PHILIP?

A. He was not one of the apostles.

B. He was a deacon. Acts 6:5. He had the qualifications of a deacon. Acts 6:3.

C. He was a soul-winner. Acts 8:1-8.

II. WHY COULD GOD USE THIS MAN?

A. Negative — not because he was a learned man, a wealthy man, a man with personality, etc.

B. Positive — because he was:

1. Obedient. Acts 8:26. He was open to divine guidance. (Note: There are two definite acts of obedience. Acts 8:26, 29.)

2. He knew his Bible. Acts 8:30-35.

3. He knew his Lord. Isa. 53, cf. Acts 8:35.

III. THE RESULTS OF THIS MEETING.

A. A man was saved who would no doubt have been lost had not Philip obeyed God.

B. God's witness of the gospel was spread to another nation. We never know when we win a soul to God. (Ill: Moody, Spurgeon, Scofield, Graham.)

24
Salvation
John 14:6; Luke 19:10; Heb. 2:3

INTRODUCTION. *This is a subject that is, or should be, of concern to every man. Salvation means deliverance. Note what the term, deliverance, implies.*

I. DELIVERANCE IMPLIES A LOST CONDITION.

   A. Mankind is lost. Rom. 3:23; Eccles. 7:20.

   B. Mankind has no righteousness to merit the favor of God. Isa. 64:6.

II. DELIVERANCE REVEALS A LIVING SAVIOUR. Acts 4:12.

   A. Christ died to deliver us from the penalty of sin, death. Eternal death. Rom. 6:23; Rev. 20:14-15.

   B. Christ lives to deliver us from the power of sin. I Cor. 10:13; Jude 24.

   C. Christ is coming again to deliver us from the presence of sin. Heb. 9:28.

III. DELIVERANCE DEMANDS A LASTING SECURITY. John 10:27-30.

   A. Note to whom He promises eternal life.

      1. My sheep hear — "A hearing ear."

      2. I know my sheep.

      3. They follow me. Cf. John 10:5.

25
In Times Like These
II Tim. 3:1–8; Matt. 24:36–41

INTRODUCTION. *We have a song entitled, "In Times Like These."
As I thought on this title, I began to think seriously about the times
in which we live. God's word paints a very graphic picture of these
days. A study of the Word will reveal that the times in which we live
are very much like the days that are to precede the coming again of
Christ; the last days of the "Dispensation of Grace."*

I.   THE SOCIAL AND HUMAN RELATIONSHIPS OF MAN IN
     THE LAST DAYS. II Tim. 3:1-4.
   A. Man's relationship with himself.
       1. Lovers of self — self-centeredness — This is forbidden by the
           Lord in the Word. II Cor. 5:15; Rom. 15:1-2.
       2. Pride. There are all sorts of pride; pride of face, race, re-
           ligion, etc.
   B. Man's relationship with others.
       1. Disobedient to parents. II Tim. 3:2; Eph. 6:1-4.
       2. Without natural affection. II Tim. 3:3. Parents refusing to care
           for their own. Spend money on wine, women, and song while
           own flesh and blood suffer. Some even killing children. Divorce
           courts filled (4,171,100 in 10 years — 1950-1960). Children
           killing parents.
       3. "False accusers." II Tim. 3:3. "Dispersers of those that are
           good." These two closely related.
           a. The devil will lie about good, consecrated men of God. John
               8:44. (Example: Stephen — Acts 6:11-12.)
           b. Dispersers of those that are good. Cf. John 16:1-3. This
               is something to be expected. II Tim. 3:12.

II. THE MATERIALISTIC CONDITION OF MEN IN THE LAST
     DAYS. Matt. 24:36-41.
   A. It will be a time of ordinary routine. Matt. 24:38. Interested
       only in earthly and physical things of life. Cf. Matt. 6:31-33.
   B. The coming of Christ which will close this dispensation will
       be wholly unexpected by many. Matt. 24:39.

III. THE RELIGIOUS CONDITION OF MEN IN THE LAST DAYS.
     II Tim. 3:4-5.
   A. Pleasure becomes men's god. I Tim. 3:4.
   B. Religion to many becomes a form. II Tim. 3:5. Void of real
       Holy Ghost power.
   C. A failure to contend for the faith. II Tim. 3:6-8; Rom. 16:17-20.

26
A Church
Using Its Building
Heb. 12:23–29

INTRODUCTION. *Through God's wonderful grace, we have a building that is not only spacious, but is also beautiful. Here is an important thing to remember: This building is not the church; it is a building to be used by the church. God used to dwell in buildings, tabernacles, temples, but now He indwells people. I Cor. 5:19-20.*

We need a clear vision of what the church is, and we must know what it is before we can know how it can serve God as it should.

I. WHAT THE CHURCH IS.

A. It is an organism.
  1. The church was foretold by Christ. Matt. 16:18.
  2. The church had its beginning at Pentecost. Acts 2:1-4.
  3. The church was revealed through Paul. Eph. 3:1-9.
  4. The church is the object of Christ's love. Eph. 5:25.
  5. It is this church that will be presented holy and without blemish to Christ. Eph. 5:26-27.

B. It is an organization. The word "church" is used 93 times, referring to local groups.

C. The difference between a local church and the true body of Christ.
  1. Local is temporary and can go out of existence. (Rev. 2:4-5. Universal is eternal. Matt. 16:18.
  2. Local can fail the Lord. Rev. 2:4, 16. Universal never fails. Matt. 16:18.
  3. Local can go astray and even become apostate. Rev. 3:14-19. Universal is always true. Eph. 5:26-27. Why does the local go astray? I John 2:18-20; II Peter 2:1-9. The only safeguard is staying by the Word, contending for the faith. Jude 2, 4.

II. A CHURCH CAN AND SHOULD USE ITS BUILDING FOR GOD.

A. A church can use its building as a place of prayer. Acts 2:42; Acts 4:23-31.

B. A church can use its building as a place to receive instruction from God's Word. Acts 2:42; John 10:9; II Tim. 2:15.

C. A church can use its building as a place to gather for spiritual worship and fellowship. Acts 2:42, 46.

D. A church can use its building as a base to win precious souls. Luke 14:23; Acts 13:1-4.

27
Love Produced
by the Spirit
Gal. 5:22

INTRODUCTION. *A study of the context, namely verses 16-21, will reveal at least three important truths. (1) The characteristics that make up Christian character is the fruit of the Spirit, not the work of man. (2) The unregenerated man cannot produce this character through his own efforts. (3) This character should be manifested in every believer as it was in Christ Jesus.*

We are only going to consider the first word mentioned in this cluster of fruit produced by the Holy Spirit of God in the life of the believer, the word, "love." As we do so, keep this truth in mind, "A human heart cannot produce divine love, but it can experience and share it."

I. THE LOVE PRODUCED BY THE HOLY SPIRIT IS NOT EX-PERIENCED BY THE UNSAVED. John 5:42.
   A. The words here were addressed to the religious people in Christ's day. John 5:39. (Searchers of the word.)
   B. They were void of love, because they had rejected Christ, the personification of love. John 5:40.

II. THE LOVE PRODUCED BY THE HOLY SPIRIT REACHES OUT FOR THE WHOLE WORLD.
   A. This love which is "divine" was manifested in God's love for mankind. John 3:16; I John 2:2.
   B. This love is also seen in the willingness of Christ to suffer for sinners. Heb. 2:9.
   C. This love is revealed today through the hearts of those that are saved. Rom. 5:5.

III. THE LOVE PRODUCED BY THE HOLY SPIRIT ABHORS THE PRESENT WORLD SYSTEM. I John 2:15-16.
   A. Love for this world system places us at emnity with God. James 4:4.
   B. Those with God's love in their heart will not love this world system. I John 2:15-16. Nor will they be loved by this world system. John 15:18-21.

IV. THE LOVE PRODUCED BY THE HOLY SPIRIT IS SACRI-FICIAL. II Cor. 8:9.
   A. True love will produce a sacrificial spirit in us for others. I John 3:16-17, cf. Rom. 9:1-3.
   B. When we have this kind of love in our hearts, we can rest assured that we know the love of God.

28
The Precious Promises
of God
II Peter 1:4; 3:9

INTRODUCTION. *The Word of God speaks of the precious and the sure promises of God. God's promises are to be depended upon, for He is not slack concerning His promises. Whatever God promises He will bring to pass.*

I want us to consider some of these wonderful promises.

I. FIRST, CONSIDER THE PROMISE OF SALVATION THROUGH THE LORD JESUS CHRIST. Gal. 3:22.
   A. Salvation is a universal need. Rom. 5:12 (Ill.: The rich young ruler — Luke 18:18-24.)
   B. Christ is the only one who can save.
      1. The message of John the Baptist. John 1:29, 45.
      2. The message of Peter. Acts 16:30-31.
      3. The claim of Christ. John 14:6.

II. SECOND, CONSIDER THE PROMISE OF THE HOLY SPIRIT TO THOSE WHO ARE SAVED. Acts 2:37-39.
   A. This promise is to all who believe on Christ. John 7:37-39; Acts 10:34-48.
   B. On Pentecost the Holy Spirit came to dwell in each and every believer. Luke 24:49. This was the specific promise of Christ. John 16:7, 13; Rom. 8:11-16.

III. THIRD, CONSIDER THE PROMISE OF ETERNAL LIFE IN CHRIST. I John 9-13.
   A. This teaching was ever before the early Christians. John 10:10, 27-30; Col. 3:3-4.
   B. The word teaches that we are kept by the power of God. I Peter 1:3-5; II Tim. 1:12; Jude 24.
   C. The assurance of eternal life is based solely upon the Word of God. Rom. 8:35-39; Eph. 2:5-7; Heb. 7:25; Ps. 89:27-37.

IV. FOURTH, CONSIDER THE PROMISE OF THE RETURN OF OUR LORD. John 14:1-3.
   A. This is the promise that Christ, Himself, made. John 14:1-3. Note three things:
      1. He is the One that is coming. I Thess. 4:16.
      2. He is coming to receive His own. I Thess. 4:16-17.
      3. He is coming that we might be with Him. I Thess. 4:17.
   B. This was the hope of the early church. Acts 1:10-11; I Thess. 1:9-10.
   C. This is a promise that serves as an incentive to Holy living. I John 3:1-3.

29
Nehemiah's Prayer
Neh. 1:1–2:5

INTRODUCTION. *The children of Judah had been carried into captivity by the nation, Babylon. Some of the men that had gone back to Judah came back to Shushan, the winter residence of the King of Persia. Nehemiah asked about the city of Jerusalem and the Jews in Judah.*

I. THE CONDITIONS THAT PREVAILED. Neh. 1:3.
   A. There was great affliction — very hard times.
   B. The walls were broken down, the gates burned. (This was the only means of protection.)
   C. But, far worse, "the people were in reproach."
      1. Many of our churches are in reproach.
      2. The world has no respect for us or for the God that we serve.
      3. When conditions like this prevail, the only thing we can do is to pray.

II. NEHEMIAH'S PRAYER. Neh. 1:4-11. This prayer contains six steps that can serve as a guide for us in our praying.
   A. He was in earnest. Neh. 1:4, "certain days."
   B. He knew God. Neh. 1:5, the right concept of God.
   C. He persevered in prayer. Neh. 1:6, "day and night." Luke 11:5-10.
   D. He made confession, Neh. 1:6. He said, "We have sinned." We usually say, "We have made a mistake," or "if we have sinned."
   E. He claimed God's promises. Neh. 1:8-10.
      1. "I know what you said you would do, Lord." Neh. 1:8-9.
      2. He held God to His promise. "You said it, Lord, and you must do it." Neh. 1:10.
   F. He had a desire to be consecrated unto the Lord. Neh. 1:11. "A desire to fear God."

III. HIS PRAYER WAS ANSWERED. Neh. 2:1-5.
   A. He was willing for God to use him to answer his prayer. Neh. 2:5. His request to the king was "Send me."
   B. When we pray for things to happen in the church, we should be willing to let God use us.

(I am indebted to the late Dr. Ernest Hancock for this outline.)

30
The Ministry
of Jesus Christ
Acts 10:34–43

INTRODUCTION. *The ministry of Jesus Christ should serve as an example unto all that have been called of God to pastor a church. I Cor. 11:1.*

I think that His ministry can be summed up under three headings: (1) His preaching. (2) His program. (3) His counseling. In this day we hear a great deal about all three of these in our own pastorates.

I. THE PREACHING OF JESUS. Mark 2:2.

  A. Jesus preached the Word. Mark 2:2, cf. II Tim. 4:1-2.

  B. He preached definite cardinal doctrines.
    1. Man is lost and needs the new birth. John 3:1-7.
    2. Man, in order to be saved, must:
      a. Repent. Luke 13:3, cf. Acts 17:30; 20:21.
      b. Believe. John 8:21, 24. (Must appropriate Him. John 6:56. He lost many of His followers. John 6:66.)

  C. He preached that man is to make Him Lord in his life. Luke 6:46-49, cf. Rom. 10:9-10.

  D. The preaching of Jesus Christ brought opposition.
    1. Accused of being born of fornication. John 8:34-41 (Vs. 41 — The implication is that they believed that Christ was born of fornication.)
    2. Accused of being a drunkard. Matt. 11:16-19.
    3. Accused of being demon possessed. Matt. 12:22-24.

II. CHRIST HAD A DEFINITE PROGRAM.

  A. A program of evangelism. Luke 10:1-2, cf. Mark 16:15-16. (Should begin at home. Eph. 6:1-4; Acts 16:31.)

  B. A program of teaching. Matt. 28:20. (Ill.: Paul — Acts 20:17-20.)

  C. A program of ministering to those in need. Acts 10:38.

III. HE GAVE COUNSEL — MANY IN OUR CHURCHES NEED COUNSELING.

  A. Those with a persecution complex. Matt. 5:11-12, 44.

  B. Those with the loyalty problem. Matt. 6:33.

  C. Those with the problem of giving. Matt. 22:21; 23:23. Jesus watched the offering plate. Mark 12:41-44.

31
The Psalm of Salvation
Ps. 32:1–11

INTRODUCTION. *This is one of the Psalms of David, the man after God's own heart. It is a Psalm that sets forth salvation by grace through faith. Paul quotes from it in Romans 4:5-8 in describing justification by faith. The Psalm divides itself into three parts, and gives a real insight into the truth of salvation.*

I. THE NEED OF SALVATION. Ps. 32:1-2.

  A. Sin is implied. Mankind is sinful. Note the terms, "transgression," "sin" — missing the mark "iniquity" — the nature.

  B. Sin is discovered, vs. 4. God's hand was upon him convicting of sin.

II. THE WAY OF SALVATION. Ps. 32:5-6.

  A. Sin is acknowledged. Ps. 32:5, cf. Ps. 51:3.

  B. Sin is confessed, vs. 5. (Confessed to God. Cf. I John 1:9) I Tim. 2:5.

  C. Sin is forgiven. Ps. 32:5. "Thou forgavest." God is a God of forgiveness. Cf. John 8:1-11. When He forgives, worry about no other. Rom. 8:33-34.

III. THE RESULTS OF SALVATION. Ps. 32:7-11.

  A. Provides a door of prayer, access to God. vs. 6.

  B. Provides a place of safety and security. vss. 6, 7, cf. Col. 3:3.

  C. Provides a guide to instruct and lead. vss. 8, 9, cf. John 16:12-15. We need to be obedient. I Peter 1:13-16.

  D. Provides a reason for rejoicing. Ps. 3:10-11. Be glad in the Lord. Cf. Isa. 61:10.

32
The Death of Lazarus
John 11

INTRODUCTION. *The death and resurrection of Lazarus is a picture of what Christ will do for us when we believe on Him as Saviour and Lord.*

I. LAZARUS WAS DEAD. John 11:14; Eph. 2:1-5.

II. LAZARUS WAS CORRUPTED. John 11:39, cf. Rom. 1:18-32; Titus 3:3.

III. JESUS LOVED HIM. John 11:5.
He loves all sinners. Rom. 5:6, 8.
I Cor. 15:3. A sinner must die for his sins, or have a sinless substitute die for him.

IV. JESUS RAISED HIM FROM THE DEAD. John 11:44.
A twofold miracle takes place when Jesus saves a sinner.

   A. Rom. 6:5. The moment the sinner believes, he is ingrafted into Christ. James 1:21, cf. John 5:39-40; Col. 3:3.

   B. The resurrection life is to flow out. John 11:44. "Loose him and let him go." The grave clothes of the old nature are to be put off. Eph. 4:22-24; Col. 3:1-4, 17.

V. JESUS FEASTED WITH THE RESURRECTED LAZARUS. John 12:1-2. Fellowship — I John 1:7.

VI. THE RESURRECTED LAZARUS WAS A TESTIMONY TO THE SAVING GRACE OF CHRIST. John 12:9-11.

33
Spiritual Power
Acts 3:1-19

INTRODUCTION. *When we come to Acts 3, we see the church rejoicing in Christ; they are witnessing to everyone they touch, and winning many souls to Christ. In this environment we see*:

I. FIRST, THE FAITHFULNESS OF GOD'S SERVANTS. Acts 3:1.
   A. Peter and John (leaders) went up to the temple to pray.
   B. These men were teaming up in God's work — "went up together," Acts 3:1. They were vastly different in many ways (age, temperament) but they were willing to work together. Why? Because in their hearts they both loved Christ.

II. SECOND, THE CONDITION OF THE SINNER. ACTS 3:1-3.
   A. Acts 3:2 tells of a crippled man, who is a very picture of the sinner in many respects.
   B. Note the comparisons:
      1. First, he was lame from birth; we are sinners from birth. Rom. 3:23; Ps. 51:5.
      2. Second, he was helpless (was carried). The sinner is helpless in that he cannot save himself. Titus 3:5; Eph. 2:8-9.
      3. Third, he had lived a dreary life. So it is with the sinner. Isa. 57:20-21.
   C. This man asked for help. Acts 3:3. Many sinners today are asking and wanting help. They are saying to the world, "My heart is empty, and I am hungry for peace and joy."
      1. The world does not have the answer.
      2. We, who know Christ, have the answer. Matt. 11:28-30; John 4:14; 6:35.

III. THE MESSAGE PROCLAIMED. Acts 3:4-6.
   A. "Look on us" These men had something to offer because they knew Christ. They could point him to Christ. John 1:29.
   B. They had power to heal. Acts 3:5-7. They were channels of God's power.

IV. THE TESTIMONY PRESENTED. Acts 3:8-19.
   A. He entered the temple, the place of worship. Saved people love the church.
   B. He was walking, leaping, praising God. A new set of legs. Acts 3:8-9. We, who are saved, have something to rejoice about. Isa. 61:10.
   C. The people were amazed. Acts 3:10-11.
   D. Gave Peter the opportunity to witness for Christ. Acts 3:12-19.

34
Shall We Continue in Sin?
Rom. 6:1

INTRODUCTION. *In the first few verses of this sixth chapter of Romans, Paul explains the meaning of baptism. I believe the Bible teaches the eternal security of the believer, but I do not believe in the believer continuing in the practice of sin. I John 3:9. This verse teaches that the believer does not practice the sin principle. It is not the order of his life to continue in sin.*

I. SHALL WE CONTINUE IN SIN WHEN WE KNOW ITS ORIGIN?
   A. Sin had its beginning in Heaven, the place of the Holy and Pure. Sin began in rebellion against God. Isa. 14:12-15.
   B. There was war in Heaven, led by the devil and his angels. Rev. 12:7-9.
   C. Sin is a terrible monster, a dreadful and deadly disease, and because of sin a curse is placed upon the human race.
   D. The first expression of sin *on the earth* was in the Garden of Eden. Gen. 3.

II. SHALL WE CONTINUE IN SIN WHEN WE KNOW ITS HISTORY?
   A. Some histories are interesting and worthwhile, but the history of sin is dark and dreadful.
   B. Sin began in defiance against God. "Hath God said." Gen. 3:1.
   C. May our hearts be turned away from sin as we see its history of shame and disgrace.

III. SHALL WE CONTINUE IN SIN WHEN WE KNOW ITS TREND?
   A. The trend of sin has always been, and is, and always shall be downward.
   B. Nations have gone down in defeat because of sin.
   C. Great leaders, in the eyes of their own nation, have gone down because of sin.

IV. SHALL WE CONTINUE IN SIN WHEN WE KNOW ITS RESULTS?
   A. Broken homes, ruined lives and character are the results of sin.
   B. "The wages of sin is death" Rom. 6:23; Gal. 6:7.

V. SHALL WE CONTINUE IN SIN WHEN WE KNOW ITS REMEDY? Isa. 1:18 John 3:14.

(I am indebted to Rev. Robert Taylor of Lewisville, N. C., for this outline.)

35
Three Classes
Among the Lost
Acts 17:30–32

INTRODUCTION. *The Word of God makes it plain that all mankind out of Christ are lost. But there are different classes among this vast multitude. I want us to consider at least three of these classes. The purpose for doing so is, that we might cause some that belong to these classes to think upon their way, and to turn unto God before it is too late.*

I. FIRST, THERE ARE THE NEGLECTORS. Heb. 2:3.

    A. All that one has to do to be eternally lost is just to do nothing about being saved. John 3:18.

    B. This is true because:

        1. Man by nature is a sinner and is lost. Rom. 5:12.

        2. As a sinner he is unfit for heaven. Rev. 22:10-15. And cannot enter in. Rev. 21:27.

        3. As a sinner he is sure of hell. John 8:21, 24.

II. SECOND, THERE ARE THE REJECTORS. A REJECTOR IS ONE WHO THINKS HE IS GOOD ENOUGH, AND DOES NOT REQUIRE ANYTHING FROM CHRIST.

    A. This was true of many Jews in the days of Paul. Rom. 10:1-3.

    B. This is illustrated in Matthew 22:9-14.

        1. The man without the wedding garment has deliberately refused the garment.

        2. He is a type of those that would be saved by their own doing. Cf. Titus 3:5.

    C. To be saved we must accept God's righteousness. Rom. 4:1-8.

III. THIRD, THERE ARE THE DESPISERS. Acts 17:32-33.

    A. These are those that "mock" at the gospel. Acts 17:32.

        1. Those that ridicule the miraculous, such as the resurrection from the dead.

        2. Those that consider themselves to be wiser than God and His word. I Cor. 3:19-20. Cf. I Cor. 1:18-21.

    B. Sinners that neglect, reject and despise can be saved only if they would turn to Christ before it is too late. John 1:12.

36
The Supreme Task
of the Church
Mark 16:14–16

INTRODUCTION. *The supreme task of the New Testament church is that of winning souls to Christ. There are many activities in the church, but they have no right to exist unless their aim is to aid in the winning of souls and building up these souls in the faith in Christ. Soul-winning is the business of the church.*

I. THIS SUPREME TASK WAS GIVEN TO THE CHURCH BY CHRIST, THE FOUNDER AND OWNER OF THE CHURCH.

   A. This is the task He gave the church to do. Mark 16:14-16.

   B. This task is to be the work of every believer. Acts 1:8; Ps. 107:2-7.

II. THERE ARE HINDRANCES THAT KEEP THE CHURCH FROM CARRYING OUT THIS SUPREME TASK.

   A. Hypocrisy, Matt. 23:27-28, tells us what a hypocrite is. Matthew 23:13 tells us what he does.

   B. Unfaithfulness. I Cor. 4:2; Mal. 2:8. Those who are saved hinder soul-winning by being unfaithful. I Tim. 4:16. (Note Paul. Phil. 1:21.)

   C. Lack of concern. Ps. 142:4. This is true today, shown by the lives of many. Note Jesus' concern. Matt. 9:35-38.

   D. Lack of vision. Prov. 29:18. A vision of lost souls on the road to to hell. John 4:35. (Ill.: D. L. Moody filled a pew of unsaved people.)

III. THERE ARE HELPS TO SOUL-WINNING.

   A. Devotion to Christ. John 14:15, 21, 23; Matt. 4:19.
      1. Something to do, "Follow me."
      2. Something for Him to do, "I will make you. . . ."

   B. Separation or consecration. Rom. 12:1-2; Col. 3:1-2. Not just hard cold separation, but a warm living sacrifice to God, taken up with love for Him.

   C. Surrender to service. John 15:16; Ps. 126:6.
      1. Prayer. Acts 1:14.
      2. Witnessing by life and word. Acts 2:4, 6, 32.

37
The Wounds of Jesus
Luke 24:36–40

INTRODUCTION. *We that are saved by the wonderful and marvelous grace of God are looking forward to the day when our wounds, blemishes, and sickness shall be removed. But the wounds of the Son of God shall ever remain. Rev. 5:6.*

Why did the Son of God allow these wounds or scars to remain? He has power to erase them. These wounds were marks of His passion, His suffering for you and for me.

Note with me what these wounds have done and will do.

I. FIRST, THEY HAD GREAT INFLUENCE UPON HIS DISCIPLES.
   A. They established His identity. Luke 24:36-40.
   B. "It is I myself" (vs. 39). The same Christ they had deserted.
   C. They were the means of convincing Thomas. John 20:24-29.

II. SECOND, HIS WOUNDS WILL BE THE THEME OF ETERNAL WONDER TO THE ANGELS.
   A. They saw Him leave heaven, and had gone with Him as far as possible, singing at His birth.
   B. Some watched while He was here upon the earth. I Tim. 3:16.
   C. When He returned, they must have crowded around Him asking, "What are these wounds in thy hands?" Zech. 13:6.

III. THIRD, THESE WOUNDS ARE HIS TROPHIES.
   A. Men win trophies for various reasons in this life: In the sports world, in the world of stage, movies, television, in the world of business and profession; even in war. Ill.: The Purple Heart.
   B. The wounds of Christ are His trophies of victory.
      1. Over death. Rev. 1:17-18, cf. I Cor. 16:54-55.
      2. Over sin. Rom. 4:25.
      3. Over Satan. Heb. 2:14-15, cf. I Cor. 10:13.

IV. FOURTH, THESE WOUNDS GUARANTEE A JUDGMENT.
   A. Man is guilty of crucifing the Son of God. Acts 2:22-24.
   B. It is this resurrected Christ with His wounds that will judge. John 5:26-27. And those who have rejected Him will be damned. John 3:18, 36, cf. Rev. 20:14-15.

(Adapted from a sermon by the Rev. Dr. Tom Malone.)

38
Positive Salvation
I John 3:14; II Tim. 1:12; Jude 24

INTRODUCTION. *The Bible is the only book that is an absolute authority on salvation. The Word of God reveals to us how to be saved, and it also reveals how we can know that we are saved. To be saved and to know it is the greatest blessing that can come to man.*
In order to be saved and to know it:

I. WE MUST KNOW THAT SALVATION HAS BEEN PROVIDED FOR US.

    A. Christ paid the redemption price. I Tim. 2:4-6; Heb. 2:9.

    B. It is God's will that we be saved. II Peter 3:9.

    C. This salvation is for everyone. Rev. 22:17.

II. WE MUST KNOW AND MEET THE CONDITIONS OF SALVATION.

    A. One must repent of his sins. Luke 13:3, 5; Acts 17:30. The forsaking of sin. Isa. 55:6-7.

    B. One must have faith in Christ for salvation. Acts 16:30; John 6:47.

III. WE MUST KNOW THAT OUR LIVES CORRESPOND TO THE WORD OF GOD.

    A. We are new creatures. II Cor. 5:17.

    B. We are free from the bondage of sin. Rom. 6:12, 22.

    C. We must love the brethren (church). I John 3:14; Gal. 6:10.

    D. We must love and obey the truth. I John 2:3-5; Ps. 119:129-131.

    E. We must love the house of God. Ps. 26:8; 84:10; 122:1; Heb. 10:24, 25.

    F. We must love everyone, even our enemies. Matt. 5:44-47.

39
The Poverty of God
Mal. 3:10

INTRODUCTION. *We must admit our text conflicts with our conception of God. To what do you suppose God had reference here in speaking of a food shortage in His house? Let us notice three things concerning the poverty of God.*

I. THE FACT OF GOD'S POVERTY.

   A. It is seen in the church finance system. Many churches have a difficult time in meeting their financial obligations; they just get by. Our text says, "a house without food" or a house without sufficient food.

   B. Many of our churches are weak in their missionary program because of a food shortage in the house of God.

II. THE CAUSE OF GOD'S POVERTY.

   A. God was rich and became poor in order to make us rich. II Cor. 8:9-12.

   B. He made us stewards of His great world riches. Christians are not putting God first in all things. Too often we serve God with our leftovers.

   C. We need to serve God with the first fruits of our increase. Matt. 6:33.

III. THE CURE FOR GOD'S POVERTY.

   A. Just treat God as you would have Him treat you.

   B. Regardless of how much or how little we make we should not *pay* less than the tithe. Mal. 3:10.

Conclusion: We receive the rich blessings of God in return for the dedication of ourselves and our means to Him. God's children have made Him a God of poverty by stealing from Him. Mal. 3:8.

(I am indebted to Rev. Robert Taylor of Lewisville, N. C., for this outline.)

40
God's Final Appeal
Isa. 1:1-20

INTRODUCTION. *God's warning to the nation of Judah is a very timely message for the church of today. The church has two things in common with Judah. (1) The condition of the church today is similar to the condition of Judah in the day of Isaiah. (2) Judah was God's chosen people. Cf. Deut.* 14:1-2 w/ *I Peter* 2:9.

I. THE CHARGE GOD MADE AGAINST JUDAH. Isa. 1:1-3.
   A. The witnesses called to witness the charge. Isa. 1:2.
   B. The charge, rebellion, vs. 2; inconsideration, vs. 3.

II. THE CONDITION THAT PREVAILED IN JUDAH. Isa. 1:4-15.
   A. Their spiritual condition before God. Isa. 1:4-9.
   B. Their religious condition before God. Isa. 1:10-15.

III. THE CORRECTION THAT NEEDED TO BE MADE BY JUDAH. Isa. 1:16-17.
   A. Wash — be cleansed from present sins. Isa. 1:16.
   B. Put away evil doings, vs. 16. Having to do with present way of life.
   C. Learn to do well. Isa. 1:17. In four distinct fields:
      1. Seek judgment. Today's two systems of judgment: one for rich, another for poor.
      2. Relieve the oppressed, the poor, the down-trodden — neglected today.
      3. Judge the fatherless.
      4. Plead for the widows. God would have us to aid and help the orphans and the widows. Cf. Exod. 22:22-24.

IV. GOD'S FINAL APPEAL TO JUDAH. Isa. 1:18-20.
   A. God gives Judah one final opportunity. Isa. 1:18. (Application to sinner.)
   B. The results if Judah heeds, vs. 19.
   C. The results if Judah ignores or disregards, vs. 20. (Applies to church).

41
A Glorious Fact,
a Tragic Decision,
and the Certain Results
Prov. 29:1

I. A GLORIOUS FACT — "BEING OFTEN REPROVED." This verse of Scripture teaches us that God deals with man in mercy before He deals with him in judgment.

   A. God reproves man through creation.

   B. God reproves man through his conscience.

   C. God reproves man through or by the Holy Spirit.

   D. God reproves man by the Word of God.

II. A TRAGIC DECISION — "HARDENETH HIS NECK."

   A. It is a personal decision; the person being often reproved makes his own decision.

   B. It is a premeditated decision.

   C. It is a pathetic decision.

   D. It is a costly decision.

   E. It is a permanent decision. D. L. Moody said, "As we live we die, and as we die we live for Eternity."

   F. It is a punishable decision. Cf. Luke 16:19-31.

III. THE CERTAIN RESULTS — "SHALL SUDDENLY BE DESTROYED."

   A. The results will be sure, "shall be."

   B. The results shall be sudden, "suddenly."

   C. The results shall be complete, "destroyed."

   D. The results shall be unavoidable, "without remedy."

CONCLUSION: What will you do with Jesus now? You are now making a decision that may seal your destiny for all eternity.

(I am indebted to Rev. Robert Taylor of Lewisville, N. C., for this outline.)

42
Blinded by Satan
II Cor. 4:3–6

INTRODUCTION. *There are multiplied thousands of people in this world that are spiritually blind and are unable to see the goodness, the grace, and the salvation of God.*

Our Scripture declares unto us that it is the work of Satan to keep people blind to the glorious gospel of Christ that is able to set them free from the power of sin.

Now, to what does Satan blind men?

I. FIRST, SATAN BLINDS MEN TO THE GOODNESS OF GOD.
   A. God's mercies are extended to us every day of our lives. Lam. 3:23.
   B. Yet, there are many that ignore, and actually hold the mercies of God in contempt. Rom. 2:4-5.
   C. The mercies of God have been abundantly bestowed upon the people of the United States. (Prosperity, freedom, etc.)

II. SECOND, SATAN BLINDS MEN TO THEIR SPIRITUAL CONDITION.
   A. Satan would lead men to believe that they are all right because they appear to be so outwardly. Matt. 23:27-28. God looks on the heart.
   B. What, then, is the condition of the lost man before God?
      1. He is a sinner. Rom. 3:23; 5:12.
      2. His best is as filthy rags before God. Isa. 65:6.
      3. He abides under the wrath of a "sin-hating God." John 3:36.

III. SATAN BLINDS MEN TO THE BIBLE TRUTH AND WAY OF SALVATION. II Cor. 4:3-4.
   A. Satan does not want men to believe the gospel of Christ. Why?
      1. Because the gospel is good news for the poor lost sinner. I Cor. 15:3-4; Rom. 5:6.
      2. Because the gospel is the power of God unto salvation. Rom. 1:14-16.
      3. Because the gospel will transform the servant of Satan into a servant of God. Rom. 6:16-18. (Ill.: the Philippian jailor.)

IV. SATAN BLINDS MEN TO THE BREVITY OF LIFE AND THE CERTAINTY OF JUDGMENT.
   A. God's word declares:
      1. That death is certain. Heb. 9:27.
      2. That life is brief. James 4:14.
      3. That we have no promise of tomorrow. Prov. 27:1.
   B. God's word also declares that all sinners shall be judged and cast into the Lake of Fire. Rev. 20:11-15; 21:8.

43
The Demands
of Discipleship
John 8:31–32

INTRODUCTION. *Jesus Christ has no use in His army for any person who does not bear the marks of the born-again, and who does not meet His demands for discipleship, no matter who that person might be. In our text, we see an important qualification set forth. "If ye continue in my Word"; this is what Christ said, and even the last portion of the verse is based upon the words just read. You cannot know the truth or be a genuine disciple of Christ unless you continue in His Word.*

I. HIS ATTITUDE TOWARD FAMILY AND SELF. Luke 14:26.

   A. The first commandment is enjoined here. Exod. 20:3.

      1. He is not teaching hatred. The word is one of comparison; it means to love less. God is to be our first and supreme love. Matt. 10:37, cf. Deut. 13:6-10.

      2. The word of God teaches us that we are to love our parents, wives and children. (This is one thing that is not true of many today. II Tim. 3:2-3.) The teaching is demonstrated in the life of Christ. Luke 2:48-49; Matt. 12:47-50.

   B. The second truth enjoined is that we are not to allow self to come first; things like education, personal pleasure, and personal gain.

II. THE ATTITUDE TOWARD SACRIFICAL SERVICE. Luke 14:27.

   A. The cross speaks of sacrifice. (Ill.: Jesus: also for another. Rom. 12:1-2.

   B. The cross speaks of suffering. This, too, is suffering for another. I Peter 2:21-24. Now we are to suffer for Him. I Peter 4:14, 16.

III. THE ATTITUDE TOWARD POSSESSIONS. Luke 14:33.

   A. The word "forsaketh" means to arrange yourself away from or off. Be not tied down to that which is material and temporal to the extent that you cannot serve Christ. I Cor. 3:11. The foundation is Christ.

   B. Count the cost. It costs to be a disciple of Christ, but just remember, it pays well in the eternity to come.

44
The Greatness of Salvation
Heb. 2:3

INTRODUCTION. *This verse of Scripture is one of God's warnings to the sinner. The road to hell is lined with such signs of mercy, put there by the Lord, that sinners might repent and be saved.*

I. WHY IS THIS SALVATION GREAT?
   A. Because of its cost.
      1. It cost God His only begotten Son. Gal. 4:4-5; Rom. 8:32.
      2. It cost Jesus Christ intense suffering at the hands of a Holy God.
         a. Christ foreknew that He would suffer. Matt. 20:17-19.
         b. Christ foreknew that He would die and spend three days in the heart of the earth. Matt. 12:38-40.
         c. This knowledge did not lessen the suffering. Matt. 26:36-38; 27:45-46.
   B. Because of its contents.
      1. It takes care of all our sins; past, present, future. Acts 13:38-39; Titus 2:14.
      2. It gives the believer the indwelling presence of the Holy Spirit. John 7:37-39.
      3. It gives the believer God's seal, which is God's pledge, the believer's assurance. Eph. 1:13-14.
   C. Because of the freedom of its conditions.
      1. Despite its cost, it is offered to us without price. Isa. 55:1-2; Rev. 22:17.
      2. The invitation is to all mankind from all walks of life. Rev. 22:17.

II. WHY DO PEOPLE NEGLECT?
   A. Because of iniquity, love for sin and its pleasures. John 3:19.
   B. Because of ignorance. Prov. 14:12.
      1. Many are ignorant of God's plan of salvation. Rom. 10:1-4.
      2. Some are ignorant of their sinfulness. Prov. 30:12.
   C. Because of indecision — putting off salvation. Prov. 1:24-31.

III. THE RESULTS OF SUCH NEGLECT.
   A. No escape for God. He must judge the sinner. Rom. 2:3-6.
   B. No escape for the unbeliever. Heb. 9:27; Rev. 21:8.

45
Baptism
Rom. 6:4

INTRODUCTION. *Baptism visualizes salvation. To visualize means to reproduce a reality in terms of sight. The reality of salvation is visualized in Scriptural baptism.*

I. BAPTISM VISUALIZES A BODY OF WATER.

   A. Jesus was baptized *in* the River Jordon. Mark 1:9.

   B. By this act Christ set His approval upon the ordinance.

II. BAPTISM VISUALIZES DEATH, BURIAL, AND RESURRECTION OF CHRIST.

   A. The main gospel truth. I Cor. 15:3-4.

   B. Baptism reproduces in terms of sight, Calvary's Cross, Christ's death on the Cross, His burial, and His resurrection on the third day.

   C. Though Christ had no sin, He had the sin and the sins of the world to bear. His baptism visualizes His assuming the responsibility of human guilt.

III. BAPTISM VISUALIZES THE DEATH AND THE RESURRECTION OF BELIEVERS.

   A. Baptism does not save; but it pictures what it does. Gal. 2:20; Rom. 6:4.

   B. Baptism visualizes the believer's faith in Christ, that He died for our sins, and was raised for our justification. Heb. 11:6; Rom. 4:25.

IV. BAPTISM VISUALIZES THE RESURRECTION FROM THE DEAD OF ALL BELIEVERS.

   A. Christ's future coming is visualized by the believer's baptism. I Cor. 15:52.

   B. The truth is, if we are planted together in the likeness of His death, we also shall be in the likeness of His resurrection. Rom. 6:5.

46
Honoring God
with Our Tithes
Lev. 27:30

INTRODUCTION. *This message is one of importance to every Christian who wishes to do the will of God in regard to money.*

I. THE TRAIL OF TITHING AS REVEALED IN GOD'S WORD.
    A. The paying of tithes originated with Abraham. Gen. 14:20.
    B. The tithe was promised by Jacob. Gen 28:22.
    C. The tithe was practiced by Israel and the tribe of Levi. Num. 18:24-26.
    D. The tithe was commanded by the Lord through the prophet, Malachi. Mal. 3:8-10.
    E. The paying of tithes was commended by Christ. Matt. 23:23.

II. THE BASIS OF TITHING AS TAUGHT IN GOD'S WORD.
    A. Because God is owner of all things, and paying a tithe is a means of recognizing God's ownership. Lev. 27:30-32; Ps. 24:1-2.
    B. Because God commands that we tithe, Mal. 3:10, and tithing proves man's obedience and love for God.
    C. Because there are many things of great importance that depend upon the paying of tithes, and offerings, of God's people.

III. THE MANNER IN WHICH GOD'S PEOPLE ARE TO SUP-PORT GOD'S WORK.
    A. Negatively. John 2:13-17.
        1. Not by sales, soup suppers, etc. This gives the sinner the wrong impression, does more harm than good.
        2. Not by begging on the streets, asking the gainsaying world for a handout.
    B. Positively. To have God's blessings, we must do His work in His prescribed way. (Ill.: We would not think of changing the mode of baptism.)
        1. Christian giving is one of the graces. II Cor. 8:1, 6-7.
        2. Christian giving can only be done by Christians. II Cor. 5:8; Rom. 8:8.
        3. Christian giving is for all Christians, rich or poor. II Cor. 8:1-3, 13-15; Mark 12:41-44.
        4. Christian giving is a test of sincerity and love. II Cor. 8:8.
        5. Christian giving should be proportioned to income. II Cor. 8:8-12.
        6. Christian giving should be systematically performed. I Cor. 16:1-2.

47
The Fact
of Christ's Coming
Acts 1:10–11

INTRODUCTION. *There is no fact in history more clearly established than the fact of the "first coming" of Christ. But as His first coming did not fulfill all of the prophecies associated with His coming, it is evident that there must be another "coming" to completely fulfill them.*

The second coming of Christ is important. Paul clearly distinguishes between the comings of Christ in Hebrews 9:26, 24, 28. While the first and second coming of Christ is separated by this dispensation, they are dependent upon each other. They are both needed to complete salvation. His first coming was to provide redemption for our bodies. There will be no resurrection until Christ comes. I Thess. 4:13-18; Rom. 8:23.

Now let us consider the fact of His coming.

I. THE TESTIMONIES OF HIS COMING.
   A. The testimony of Jesus Himself. Matt. 16:27; John 14:2-3; 21:22.
   B. The testimony of the heavenly beings. Acts 1:10-11.
   C. The testimony of the disciples. Phil. 3:20-21; II Peter 1:16.
   D. The testimony of the Lord's Supper. I Cor. 11:26.

II. THE THEORIES CONCERNING HIS COMING.
   A. That His coming again is "Spiritual" and was fulfilled at Pentecost.
      1. Holy Spirit came at Pentecost, not Christ. His coming conditioned on Christ's absence. John 16:7.
      2. If Holy Spirit is just another manifestation of Christ, this nullifies Trinity. Matt. 28:19.
      3. The whole of the New Testament written after Pentecost mentions Christ's coming as future over 150 times.
   B. The conversion of sinners the second coming. The sinner comes to Christ for salvation. Matt. 11:28. The second coming of Christ is visible and personal. I Thess. 4:16; Rev. 1:7.
   C. That death is the second coming.
      1. A person passes into eternity every second. Christ would be coming every second. Have to leave His High Priestly work.
      2. The fact is when a believer dies he goes to be with Christ. II Cor. 5:6-8.
      3. The disciples did not think of death as being the same thing as the second coming. John 21:21-23; Phil. 3:20-21.

48
The Manner
of His Coming
Acts 1:10–11

INTRODUCTION. *Of the exact time of Christ's coming we cannot be certain. When Jesus was on the earth He said so in Matthew 25:13. After His resurrection He refused to satisfy the curiosity of His disciples. Acts 1:7. The believer is not to be a "date-setter," but he is exhorted to watch. Mark 13:33. There is nothing to prevent Christ from coming for His church now.*

While we do not know the day or hour of Christ's coming, we do know that His coming is certain. According to the Word of God there will be two stages to His coming. One known as the rapture; the other, as the revelation.

I. SCRIPTURES SETTING FORTH THESE TWO STAGES.
   A. At the rapture: "He comes in the air." I Thess. 4:13-17. At the revelation: "He comes to the earth." Zech. 14:3-4.
   B. At the rapture: He comes as the "Morning Star." Rev. 22:16. At the revelation: He comes as the "sun of Righteousness." Mal. 4:1-2. (Note: There is darkness between the two — "Tribulation.")
   C. At the rapture: "He comes to receive His Bride, the church." John 14:3. At the revelation: He comes to be received by Israel in true repentance. Zech. 12:10.

II. THE RAPTURE, THINGS THAT WILL TAKE PLACE.
   A. The rapture will be a surprise. Matt. 24:39-44.
   B. Two important events will take place:
      1. The resurrection of the dead in Christ. John 11:25-26; Rev. 20:4-6.
      2. The translation of the living saints. I Cor. 15:51-57; I Thess. 4:15-17.
   C. The rapture will be "elective." Matt. 24:38-41.
      1. We do not know if any, except the church, will see or hear Him at His coming. Acts 1:10-11, cf. John 12:28-29 and Acts 9:3-7; cf. Acts 22:9.
      2. All believers will be taken. I Thess. 4:16-17. As a body. I Cor. 12:12-14. It will be a startling thing when this happens.

III. THE EXHORTATION GIVEN IN THE LIGHT OF THIS TRUTH. Luke 19:13. "Occupy till I come."

49
What Will Take Place
on Earth After the
Rapture of the Church?
I Thess. 4:13–18

INTRODUCTION. *We want to see, from God's Word, what is going to take place here on the earth after the true saints of God are caught up to meet the Lord. We cannot cover all that is to take place in minute detail. We want to get a bird's-eye view of the events that are to pass here on the earth after the true church is gone.*

Keep this in mind, the unbelievers are left here on earth, the unbelieving dead are still in their tombs.

I. THERE WILL BE GREAT CONSTERNATION ON EARTH.
   A. There will be the missing of all believers. Matt. 24:37-42.
   B. However, there will still be churches and professionists. Rev. 3:10, cf. Matt. 7:20-21.

II. THERE WILL BE THE MANIFESTATION OF THE ANTI-CHRIST. II Thess. 2:3, 7, 8.
   A. The nature of the Anti-Christ.
      1. He will be an imitator of the true Christ. Rev. 6:1-2, cf. Rev. 19:11-16; 13:3.
      2. He will be:
         a. A religious leader. Rev. 13:4.
         b. A political leader. Rev. 13:7.
         c. An economical leader. Rev. 13:16-17.

III. THERE WILL BE THE PERIOD KNOWN AS THE GREAT TRIBULATION.
   A. It will be a time of vengeance for our Lord. Zeph. 1:14-18.
   B. It will be a time when peace will be taken from the earth. Rev. 6:3-4.
   C. It will be a time of famine. Rev. 6:5-6.
   D. It will be a time of death for many. Rev. 6:8. For others, it will be a time when they shall seek death and cannot die. Rev. 6:15-17; 9:1-6.

IV. CAN ANYONE BE SAVED DURING THIS TIME?
   A. Many will be saved in that day. Rev. 7:9-14.
   B. But it will be hard for a person who has heard the gospel during this day to be saved in that day. II Thess. 2:11-12.

50
What Will Happen in Heaven After the Rapture of the Church?
I Cor. 4:1–5; II Cor. 5:9–10

INTRODUCTION. *There are to be two stages of His coming: the rapture and the revelation. What will take place in heaven after the believers are caught up to meet the Lord?*

I. FIRST, THERE WILL BE THE JUDGMENT SEAT OF CHRIST. II Cor. 5:10; Rom. 14:10. What does the Word teach about the Judgment Seat of Christ?
   A. Only the saved will be judged there. II Cor. 5:10. Unsaved at the White Throne. Rev. 20:11-15.
   B. The Judgment Seat will be a time of testing. I Cor. 3:11-15.
   C. It will be a time of rewards. I Cor. 3:14.
      1. The Crown of Life. James 1:12. Enduring trials.
      2. The Crown of Righteousness. II Tim. 4:8. Faithfulness in service as a result of loving the coming of Christ.
      3. The Incorruptible Crown. I Cor. 9:25. Singleness of purpose. Temperance in all things.
      4. The Crown of Glory. I Peter 5:2-4. Faithful feeding of the flock of God.
      5. The Martyr's Crown. Rev. 2:10.
      6. The Crown of Rejoicing. I Thess. 2:19-20. The soul-winner's crown. Prov. 11:30, cf. Dan. 12:3.
      7. Note Rev. 22:12; 3:11. II John vs. 8.
   D. All of God's ways with the believer will be vindicated.
      1. We will understand why God permitted trials, sickness, etc. I Cor. 13:12.
      2. This will be of minor importance when compared to the glory that is to be ours. Rom. 8:18.

II. SECOND, THERE WILL BE THE MARRIAGE SUPPER OF THE LAMB. Rev. 19:7-9.
   A. The Bride will be made ready. Rev. 19:7-8. Righteousness is the paramount virtue here.
   B. Others will be called. Rev. 19:9. The wedding guests are the Old Testament saints. The church is the bride. Eph. 5:25-27. We have much to be glad for and to rejoice over, vs. 7.
   C. Some things that are of interest about the marriage supper.
      1. We will be in perfect harmony at the supper; no discord nor strife. Rev. 19:6-7. This is the reason that I believe it will follow the Judgment Seat of Christ.
      2. The wedding bond will never be broken; not by divorce, nor by death.